Around the World in 80 Picture Puzzles

Exciting Activities, Fun Facts, and More!

Illustrated by Emma Trithart

ARCTURUS

ARCTURUS

This edition published in 2023 by Arcturus Publishing Limited
26/27 Bickels Yard, 151–153 Bermondsey Street,
London SE1 3HA

Author: Susie Rae
Illustrator: Emma Trithart
Editor: Lucy Doncaster
Designer: Nathan Balsom
Design Manager: Jessica Holliland
Editorial Manager: Joe Harris

ISBN: 978-1-3988-3114-8
CH010468NT
Supplier 29, Date 0823, PI 00003552

Printed in China

Phoebe and Felix Fogg are exploring their attic one rainy day, when they stumble on some boxes that used to belong to their great-great-grandpa, Phileas Fogg. It turns out that he was a famous explorer who went around the whole world in 80 days! They spend hours reading all about his incredible adventures in many fascinating countries. Then they have an idea! They want to follow in their ancestor's footsteps and set out on their own epic journey around the world, with their pet parrot and best friend Passepartout ... and they want you to come with them! So pack your suitcase, grab your passport, and get ready to join Phoebe, Felix, and Passepartout on the most exciting adventure of your life, discovering new things and solving some clever activities along the way.

CONTENTS

Use this page to track Felix, Phoebe, and
Passepartout's journey around the globe!

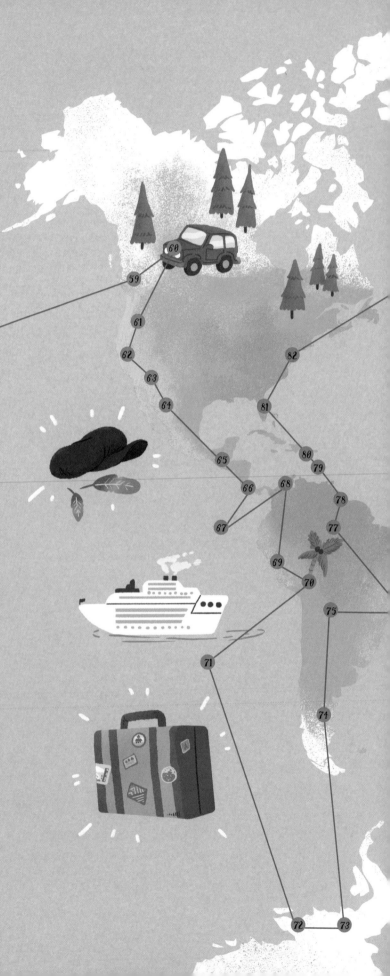

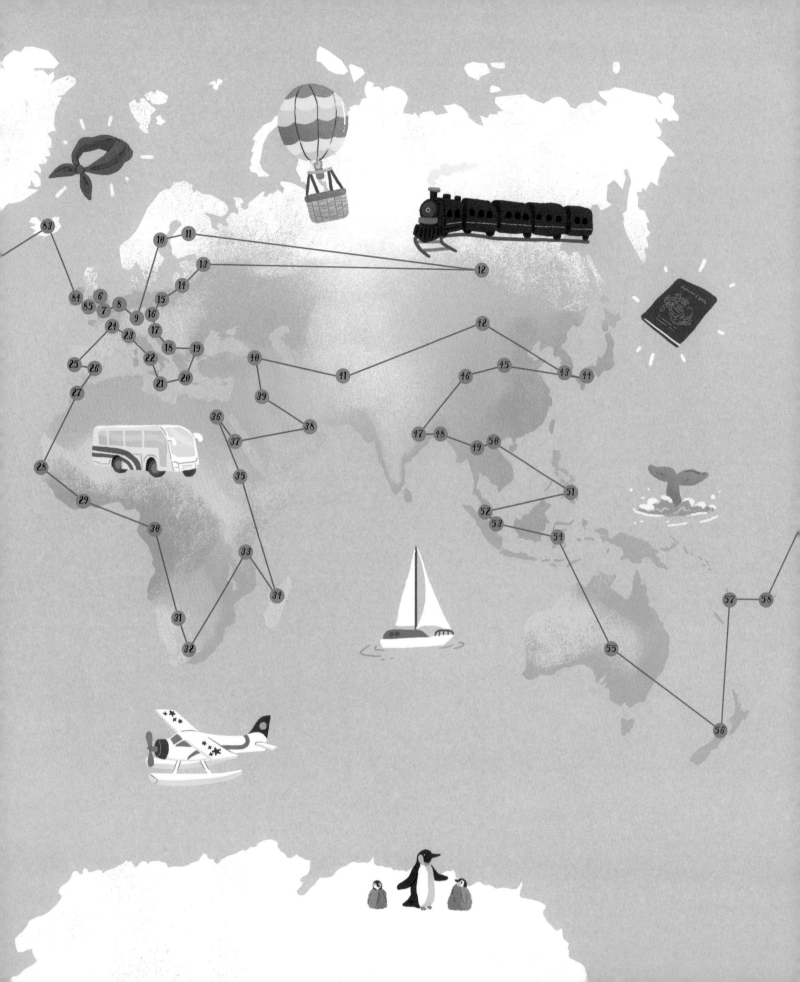

CHANGING OF THE GUARD

Phoebe, Felix, and Passepartout are watching the changing of the guard at Buckingham Palace in London, England. Can you spot ten differences between these two pictures?

England, UK

OFF THE RAILS

The children are people-watching while waiting for their train to Paris, France, from London. Are there more people with wheeled suitcases or backpacks in this busy station scene?

DUTCH DELIGHT

The children are now in the Netherlands enjoying a bicycle tour of the countryside. Join the dots to see what famous landmark they are taking photos of.

The Netherlands

FUN OF THE FAIR

Use the code below to fill in this picture of Felix, Phoebe, and Passepartout's evening at a Christmas fair in Frankfurt, Germany.

1 **2** **3** **4** **5** **6** **7** **8** **9** **10**

Germany

HORSE HUNT

In the morning, the children went shopping in Stockholm, Sweden, where they bought nine hand-painted wooden horses as souvenirs. Now they are picking cloudberries in the countryside. Felix is still holding one horse, but they've lost eight. Can you find them all?

REINDEER REVEAL

Felix, Phoebe, and Passepartout are exploring Finland, and have come to meet some friendly reindeer. Which one is ever so slightly different from its friends?

LAKE FISHING

The Fogg children and Passepartout are fishing in the cold waters of Lake Baikal in Russia with some local friends. Follow the lines to work out who has caught the fish.

STATUE MATCH

Phoebe, Felix, and Passepartout are visiting St Petersburg in Russia and are sketching some of the famous statues there. Can you spot which silhouette of the Bronze Horseman exactly matches the real statue?

ISLAND ESCAPE

Felix and Phoebe have spent the day exploring Trakai Island Castle in Lithuania. Can you help them find a path through the courtyard maze to the exit?

START

FINISH

POLISH PLATES

The Fogg children have been learning how to paint traditional Polish roosters. Can you tell which of these painted plates is different from the others?

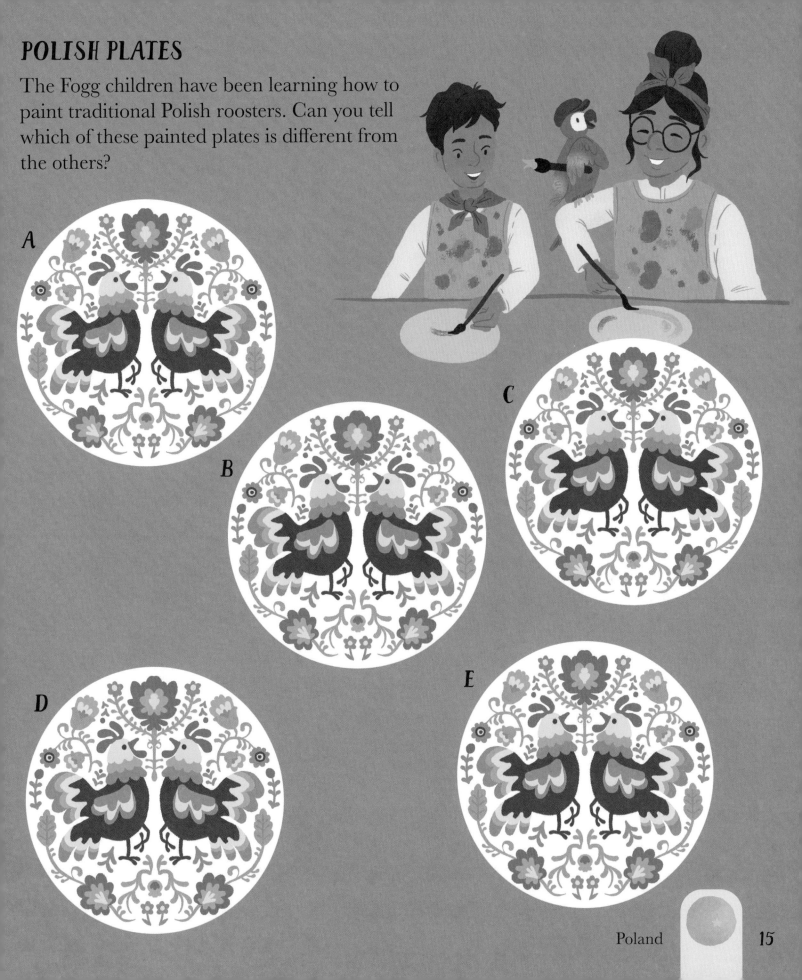

A

B

C

D

E

ON THE SPOT

Can you spot ten differences in these two photos of the Foggs at the beautiful Klementinum Library in Prague, Czech Republic?

  Czech Republic

MOUNTAIN MUDDLE

The children and Passepartout are hiking on the lower slopes of Mount Triglav in Slovenia. Complete this scene using the pieces below, then work out which one doesn't belong in the picture.

A   B   C   D   E   F   G

CROATIA CAPER

Join the dots in the correct order to see what type of transport the Foggs will be using to explore the sea around Croatia.

BRIGHT BUILDINGS

Follow the key below to shade in this picture of Sighișoara in Transylvania, Romania.

1 2 3 4 5 6 7 8 9 10

COUNT THE CATS

Felix and Phoebe are enjoying spotting wildcats in Greece, though Passepartout isn't so sure. How many wildcats can you find in this rocky shore scene?

RAINBOW SPOTTING

The Foggs are exploring in the Mediterranean Sea. Which of these bright rainbow wrasse fishes is not like the others?

CANAL CAPER

The Fogg children are enjoying a gondola ride through the canals of Venice, Italy. Can you find the right route back to Passepartout and their hotel?

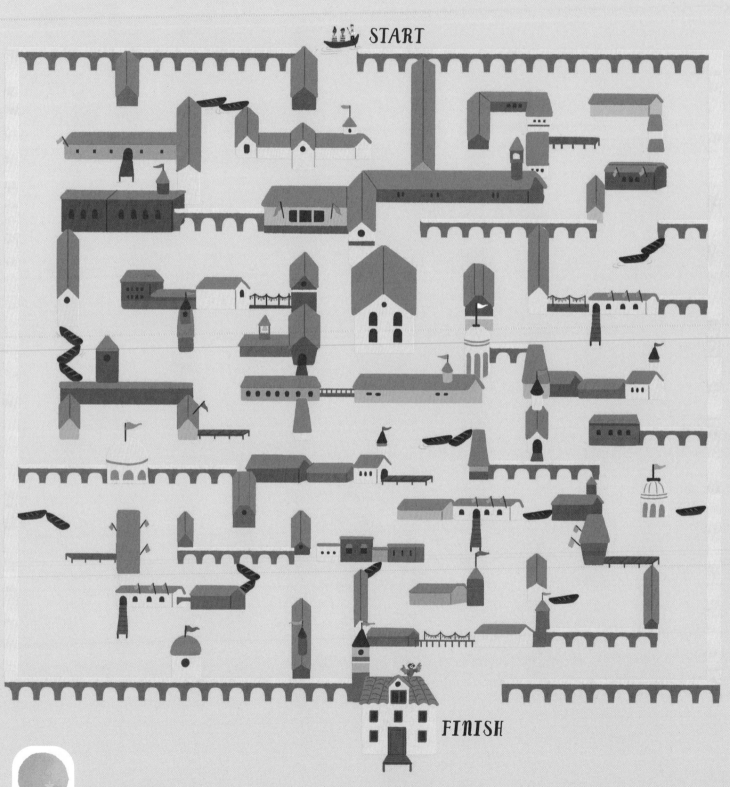

Italy

MATTERHORN MIX-UP

The Matterhorn, on the border of Switzerland and Italy, is one of the highest mountains in Europe. Can you put this picture of it back in the right order by writing the numbers in the spaces below?

1   2   3   4   5   6   7   8

—   —   —   —   —   —   —   —

Phoebe and Felix are visiting Paris, France, and are drawing some of the sights. Can you spot which silhouette of the Eiffel Tower exactly matches the real thing?

France

PALACE PUZZLER

Can you spot ten differences between these pictures of
Pena Palace in São Pedro de Penaferrim, Portugal?

RABBIT TWINS

Felix and Phoebe are hiking in the Spanish mountains, and have been charmed by the skipping rabbits. Can you find the matching pair for each rabbit below? Circle the one that doesn't have a twin.

Spain

SOUK SUDOKU

Complete this grid using the six foods sold in the souk in Marrakesh, Morocco. Can you place these items once in each column, row, and mini grid?

HIDE AND SEEK

The Foggs are on a nighttime safari in Senegal. How many bush babies can you see hiding in the trees?

Senegal

TIME FOR A KICK-ABOUT

Felix and Phoebe are playing a game with
some friends on a beach in Côte d'Ivoire.
Join the dots to discover what kind of tree
is on the beach.

MOTHERLY LOVE

Phoebe, Felix, and Passepartout have come to see okapis in the wild in the Democratic Republic of the Congo. Can you spot ten differences between these two scenes?

Democratic Republic of the Congo

ODD REFLECTION OUT

The children and Passepartout are on safari in Botswana and have come to a watering hole to watch the wildlife. Can you spot which reflection doesn't match its giraffe?

IN A STEW!

The children are enjoying a meal in South Africa. Which of these pictures of delicious potjiekos is not the same as the others?

A

B

C

D

E

A FAMILY AFFAIR

Felix, Phoebe, and Passepartout have spotted an elephant family near Mount Kilimanjaro in Tanzania. Can you work out which puzzle piece doesn't fit in the picture below?

A   B   C   D   E

CHAMELEON MATCH-UP

Felix and Phoebe have been admiring chameleons in a forest in Madagascar. Can you tell which of these silhouettes exactly matches the one they're looking at here?

A

B

C

D

F

E

KING OF THE CASTLE

The children are exploring Fasil Ghebbi, one of the biggest castles in Ethiopia. Can you put this picture back in the right order by writing the numbers in the spaces below?

1   2   3   4   5   6   7   8

—   —   —   —   —   —   —   —

MARKET MAZE

Felix and Phoebe are hungry after a busy few hours' shopping at Khan el-Khalili souk in Cairo, Egypt. Can you find the path they should take to get to the café?

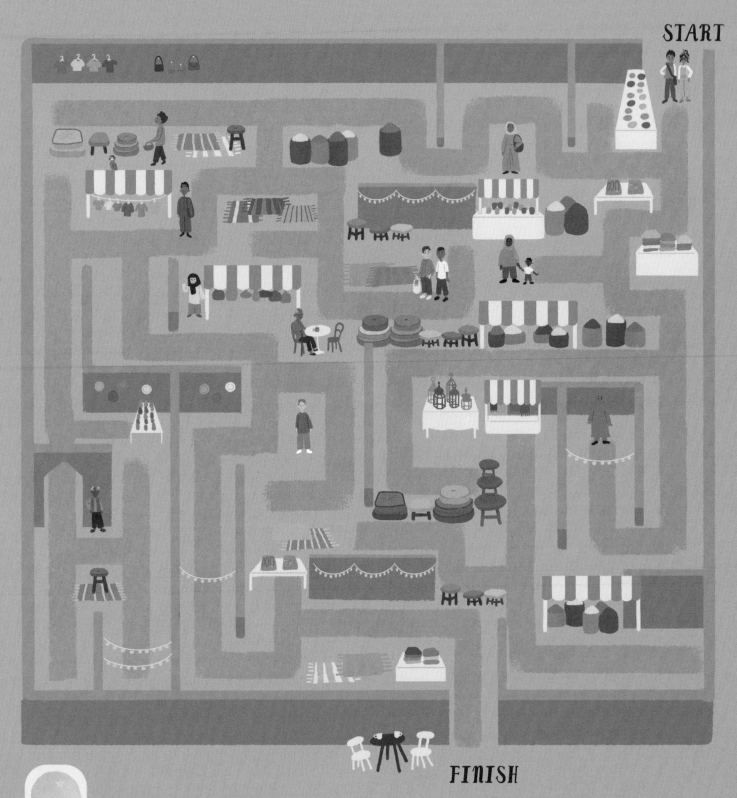

START

FINISH

Egypt

SPOT THE SCARAB

Phoebe, Felix, and Passepartout are trying to decide which ancient Egyptian carved scarab beetle they like the best. Can you find the one that doesn't have a matching pair?

MOSQUE MUDDLE

Phoebe and Felix have each taken a photo of Sheikh Zayed Grand Mosque in Abu Dhabi, United Arab Emirates (UAE). Can you spot ten differences between them?

Abu Dhabi, UAE

GOLDEN GATEWAY

Phoebe and Felix are at the reconstruction of the ancient Ishtar Gate in Iraq. Can you draw in the other half of the gate, using the grid to help you? It is an exact mirror image of the half shown.

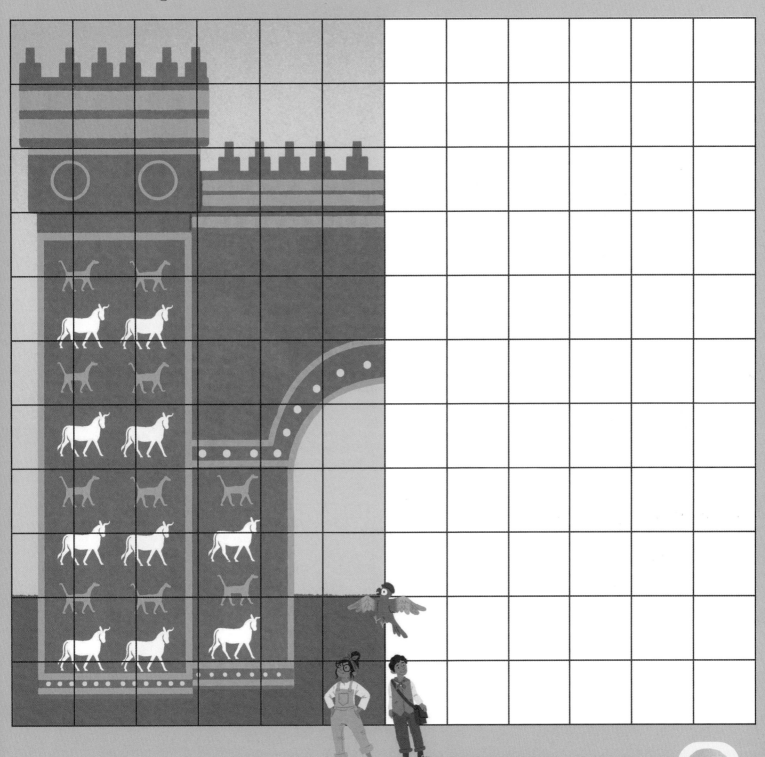

RACE TO THE BOTTOM

Which of the cable cars should the Fogg children take to get down the mountain in Khulo, Georgia?

Georgia

FEELING BLUE

Use the key to help you shade in this close-up of the Blue Mosque in Mazar-i-Sharif, Afghanistan.

1
2
3
4

GOT THE HUMP

The Fogg children are staying in a traditional tent called a ger on the Mongolian plains, sketching the wildlife. Use the grid to help you copy this picture of a Mongolian Bactrian camel.

Mongolia

TOWER TEASER

Which of these pictures of N Seoul Tower in South Korea is slightly different from the others?

A

B

C

D

E

SHRINE ISLAND

Felix and Phoebe are visiting Itsukushima Shrine on Miyajima, Japan. Can you work out which puzzle piece doesn't fit in the picture below?

A  B C  D E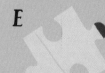

Japan

WALL OF WONDER

Phoebe and Felix have been walking along the Great Wall of China. Can you put this picture back in the right order by writing the numbers in the spaces below?

ANCIENT ARMY

The children have gone to see the Terracotta Army in Shaanxi, China. Help them follow this pattern to find their way to the other side of the exhibition, to join Passepartout, who has flown ahead. You can move up, down, left, and right, but not diagonally.

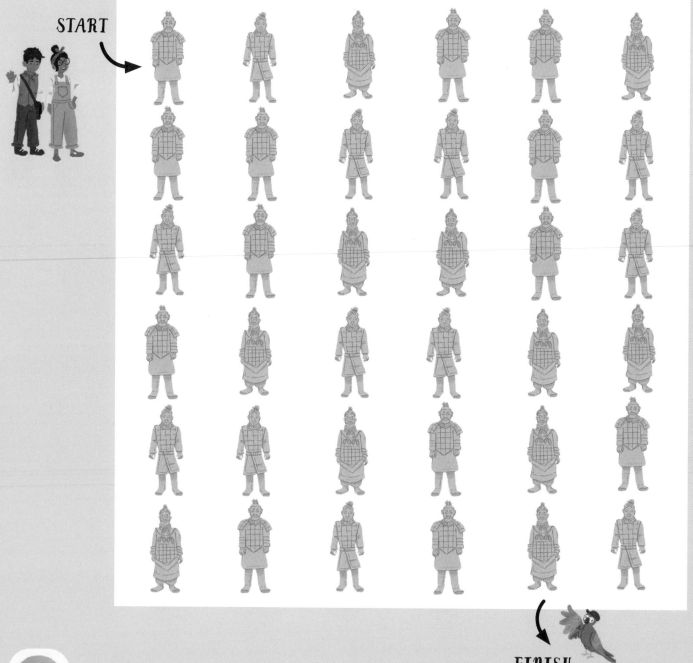

START

FINISH

China

IT'S A JUNGLE OUT THERE!

The Foggs need to find their way back to the bus on the other side of this banyan grove in India. Can you help them to find the right path? They can't walk through trees that block the path.

START

FINISH

PEACOCK PUZZLER

The Fogg children have been watching peacocks at a farm in Bangladesh. Can you find the matching pair for each peacock below? Circle the one that doesn't have a twin.

Bangladesh

TEMPLE TEASER

Felix and Phoebe are visiting the "White Temple" in Chiang Rai, Thailand. Can you spot ten differences between these selfies?

COUNT THE BOATS

The Fogg children are taking part in the Huong Pagoda Festival in northern Vietnam. Are there more blue boats or yellow boats in this busy scene?

Vietnam

BANGKA BOATING

Felix and Phoebe are going to take a bangka boat out for the day to explore the islands of the Philippines. Join the dots to see what it looks like.

BRIGHT BLOOMS

Felix, Phoebe, and Passepartout are spending a morning at the flower market in Kuala Lumpur, Malaysia. Follow the key to shade in this picture.

Malaysia

BIRD WATCHING

How many parrots, including Passepartout, can you spot in this picture of Felix and Phoebe at this bird park in Singapore?

ODD ORANGUTAN OUT

The Foggs have got their binoculars out and are watching the wildlife in Indonesia. Which of these Indonesian orangutans is different from the rest?

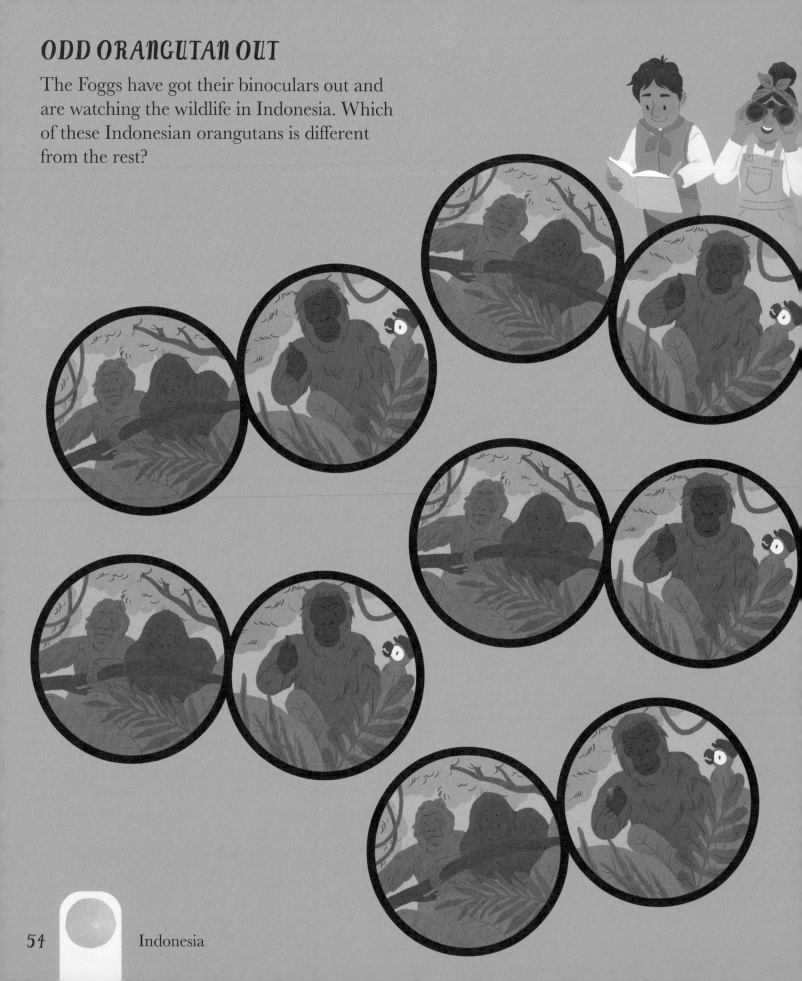

HOP TO IT

G'day from the Outback in Australia! Felix, Phoebe, and
Passepartout are watching kangaroos bounding across the bush.
Can you work out which puzzle piece doesn't fit in the picture below?

CURIOUS KĀKĀPŌS

Which of these silhouettes exactly matches
the kākāpō that Felix and Phoebe have
been watching in New Zealand?

CORAL MAZE

This brain coral from Fiji has a maze on its body! Can you find a way through?

START

FINISH

UNDERWATER ADVENTURE

The children are having fun exploring the warm waters off Bora Bora in French Polynesia, and admiring the fish and coral. Follow the key to shade in this picture.

Bora Bora, French Polynesia

TOTEM TEASER

Felix, Phoebe, and Passepartout have found the totem poles at Brockton Point, Vancouver, Canada. Can you spot ten differences between these pictures?

BEAVERING ABOUT

Which of these trails will lead the beaver back to its lodge at the edge of this lake in Alberta, Canada?

A

B

C

Alberta, Canada

BRIDGING THE GAP

The children and Passepartout are admiring Astoria–Megler Bridge in Oregon, USA.
Can you put this picture back in the right order by writing the numbers in the spaces below?

ALL ABOARD!

The children and Passepartout are planning to take a ride on a cable car to help them explore San Francisco, California in the USA. Join the dots to see what it looks like.

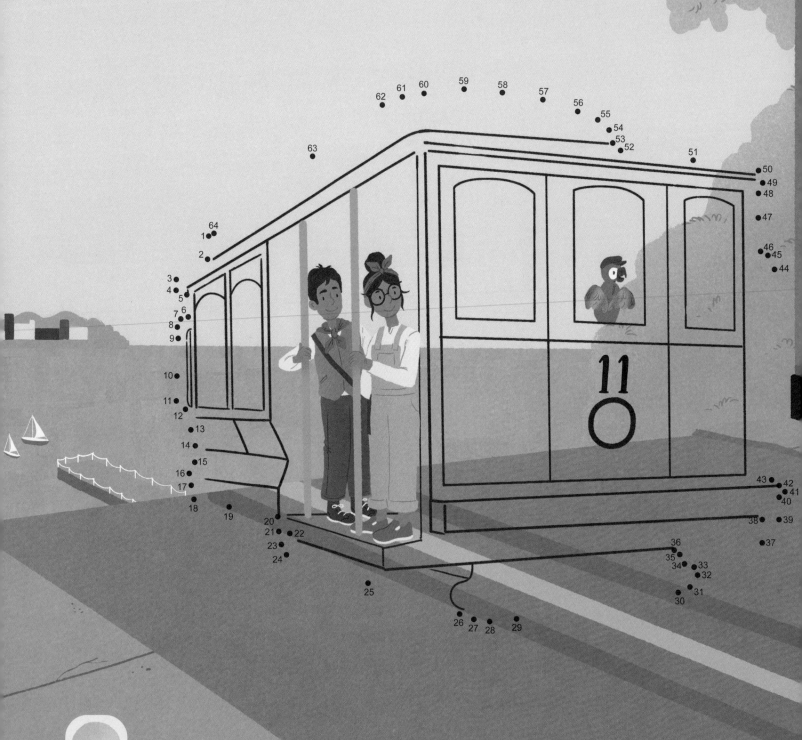

San Francisco, USA

SUNSET SPECTACULAR

As dusk descends, the children and Passepartout are admiring the view in the Arizona desert in the USA. Follow the key to shade in this picture.

Arizona, USA

LIZARD LOOKOUT

Sonoran collared lizards live in the shrubland of Sonora, Mexico. The males are a vibrant blue-green, and the females are less bright. Can you count how many females are in the picture below?

PICTURE PERFECT

Complete this picture of the children kayaking on Lake Atitlán in Guatemala, using the missing pieces at the bottom of the page. Which piece doesn't fit?

A

B

C

D

E

WATERFALL WONDER

The children and Passepartout have hiked through the rain forest to look at the bright blue water of the Río Celeste Waterfall in Costa Rica. Can you spot which of these selfies is the one odd out?

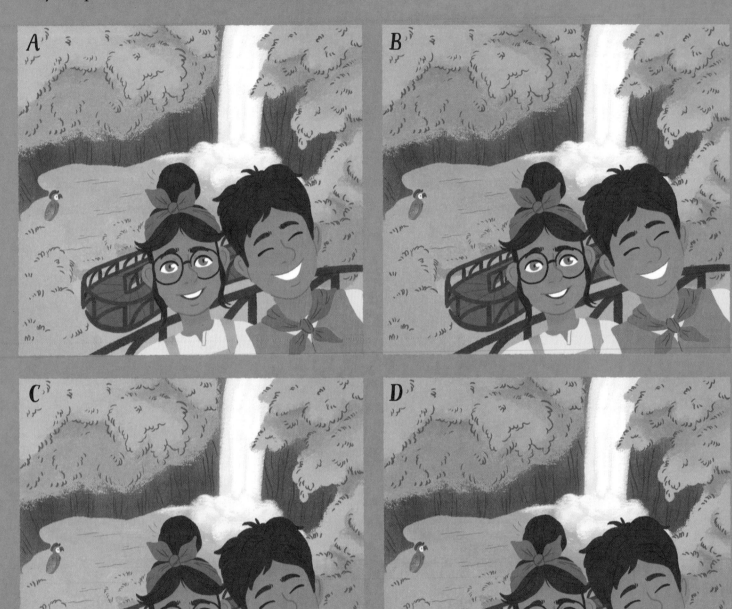

Costa Rica

FEEDING TIME!

Felix and Phoebe have been lucky enough to join the caretakers of these giant tortoises in the Galápagos Islands. Can you put this picture back in the right order by writing the numbers in the spaces below?

1　　2　　3　　4　　5　　6　　7　　8

___ ___ ___ ___ ___ ___ ___ ___

LOST CITY OF TEYUNA

Can you help Felix and Phoebe find their way to
the middle of the Lost City of Teyuna in Colombia,
so they can be reunited with Passepartout?

START

FINISH

Colombia

LLAMA LINK-UP

The Fogg children are meeting llamas in Peru.
Can you match each llama up with its pair?
Which one doesn't have an exact twin?

A PRICKLY PROBLEM

Wow! These cacti on Fish Island, Bolivia, are very tall. Can you tell which of these silhouettes exactly matches the picture above?

MOAI MUDDLE

Can you spot ten differences between these two pictures of Felix and Phoebe joining the Moai statues on Easter Island, Chile?

Easter Island, Chile

PENGUIN PANDEMONIUM

Help the Foggs count whether there are more small
Adélie penguins or large emperor penguins in this
snowy scene in Antarctica.

Antarctica

PERFECT POSING

Phoebe and Felix are exploring Antarctica and have come across these cute Antarctic fur seals. All of the selfies they have taken are identical apart from one. Can you spot the odd one out?

A

B

C

D

BRIGHT BUILDINGS

Wow! There's so much to see in the vibrant La Boca area of
Buenos Aires, Argentina. Can you put this picture back in
the right order by writing the numbers in the spaces below?

Argentina

NATURE'S RAINBOW

Felix, Phoebe, and Passepartout are still in Argentina, flying over the Fourteen Colored Mountain in a hot air balloon. Follow the key to shade in this picture.

 1   2 3 4 5 6

SELARÓN STEPS

Complete this jigsaw puzzle of Phoebe and Felix's trip to the Selarón Steps in Rio de Janeiro, Brazil, using the missing pieces at the bottom of the page. Which piece doesn't fit?

A

B

C

D

E

Brazil

JUNGLE SUDOKU

Complete this grid using the six Amazonian rain forest animals below. Can you place these animals once in each column, row, and mini grid?

KITE CATASTROPHE!

Oh dear, the kites have all got in a tangle during the annual Easter Monday kite-flying festival in Georgetown, Guyana. Following the lines, can you work out which kite belongs to each child—Phoebe, Felix, or one of their new friends?

FLYING HIGH

Barbados is known for its flying fish. Help Phoebe and Felix swim from their boat to the beach. Their route must follow the pattern below. You can move up, down, left, and right, but not diagonally.

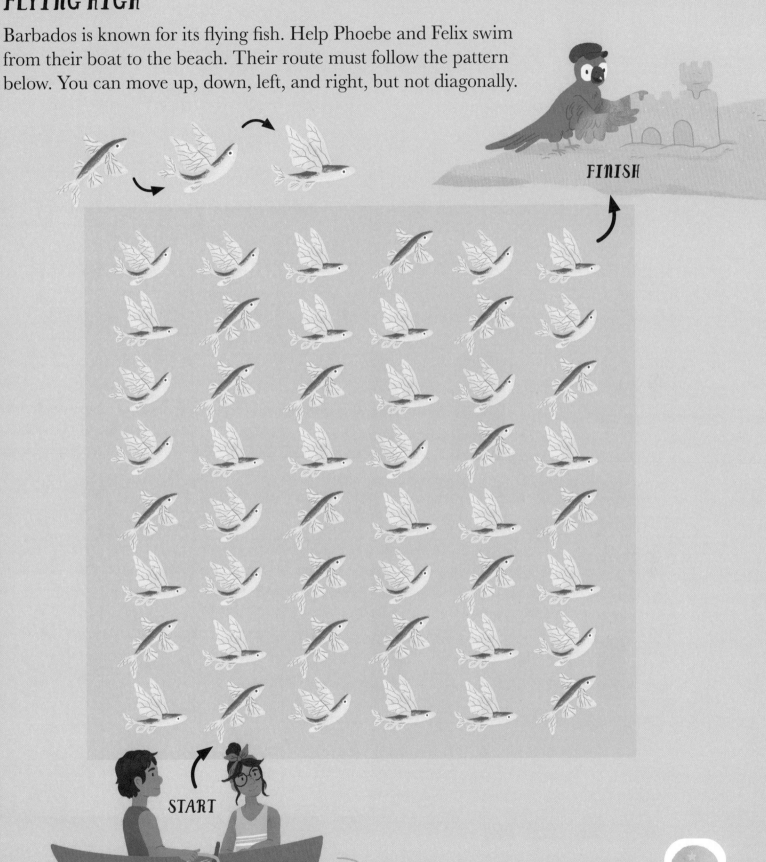

FINISH

START

MIRROR IMAGE

Cathédrale de St-Pierre et St-Paul is in the middle of Pointe-à-Pitre in Guadeloupe. Using the grid to help you, draw the rest of the building, which is a mirror image of the side already shown.

Guadeloupe

LOOK SNAPPY!

The children are watching alligators in Florida, USA. Each alligator is part of a matching pair, apart from one. Can you spot all four pairs (the alligators might be facing in different directions). Circle the odd one out.

Florida, USA

CURTAIN UP!

The children are watching a show on Broadway in New York, USA. Can you spot ten differences between these images?

New York, USA

PUFFIN PALAVER

Felix and Phoebe are exploring the coast of Iceland.
Are there more adult puffins or smaller, fluffy chicks
in this puffin colony?

PRETTY AS A PICTURE

Felix and Phoebe are in Kinsale, in the Republic of Ireland. Use your brightest pens and pencils to shade in this picture.

Republic of Ireland

ANCIENT MONUMENT

Join the dots to reveal Stonehenge, where the Foggs are watching the sun rise in southern England on their way back home to London.

PAGE 6

PAGE 7

There are 9 suitcases and 8 backpacks.

PAGE 8

The answer is a windmill.

PAGE 9

PAGE 10

PAGE 11

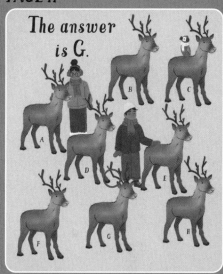

The answer is G.

PAGE 12

PAGE 13

The answer is E.

87

PAGE 14

PAGE 15

The answer is A.

PAGE 16

PAGE 17

The answer is D.

PAGE 18

The answer is a boat.

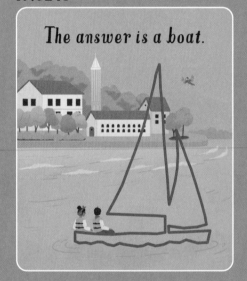

PAGE 19

PAGE 20

The answer is 10.

PAGE 21

PAGE 22

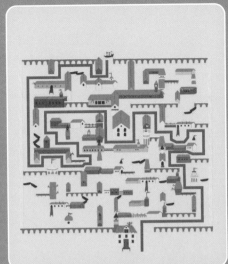

PAGE 23

3 6 1 7 5 8 4 2

PAGE 24

The answer is C.

PAGE 25

PAGE 26

The rabbit ringed in black is the odd one out.

PAGE 27

PAGE 28

The answer is 15.

PAGE 29

The answer is a palm tree.

PAGE 30

PAGE 31

The answer is D.

PAGE 32

The answer is D.

PAGE 33

The answer is C.

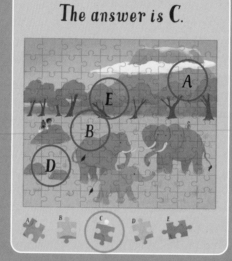

PAGE 34

The answer is D.

PAGE 35

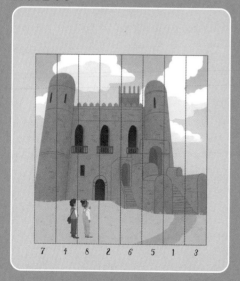

PAGE 36

PAGE 37

The beetle ringed in black is the odd one out.

PAGE 38

PAGE 40

The answer is 3.

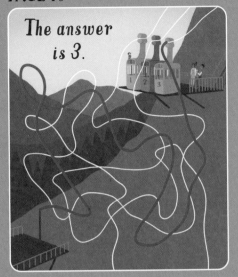

PAGE 41

PAGE 43

The answer is E.

PAGE 44

The answer is A.

PAGE 45

PAGE 46

PAGE 47

PAGE 48

The peacock ringed in black is the odd one out.

PAGE 49

PAGE 50

There are 10 blue boats and 9 yellow boats.

PAGE 51

PAGE 52

PAGE 53

There are 15 parrots.

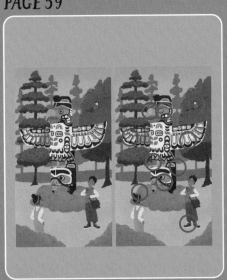

PAGE 54

PAGE 55

The answer is E.

PAGE 56

The answer is A.

PAGE 57
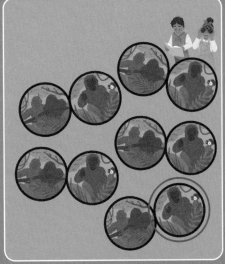

PAGE 58

PAGE 59

PAGE 60
The answer is A.

PAGE 61

PAGE 62

PAGE 63

PAGE 64

The answer is 15.

PAGE 65

The answer is C.

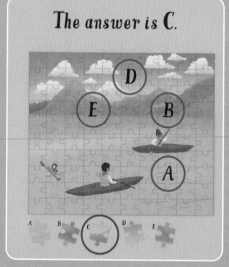

PAGE 66

The answer is B.

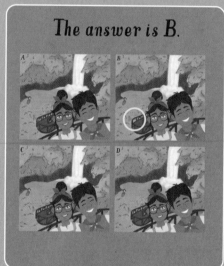

PAGE 67

2 5 8 7 3 6 1 4

PAGE 68

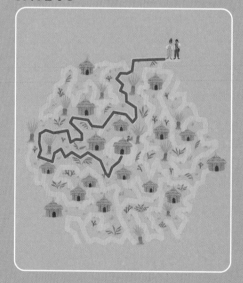

PAGE 69

The llama ringed in black is the odd one out.

94

PAGE 70

The answer is A.

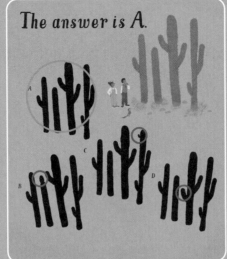

PAGE 71

PAGE 72

There are 15 Adélie penguins and 17 emperor penguins.

PAGE 73

The answer is A.

PAGE 74

PAGE 75

PAGE 76

The answer is B.

PAGE 77

PAGE 78

The answer is 1A, 2E, 3D, 4C, 5B.

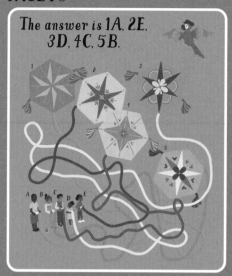

PAGE 79

PAGE 81

The alligator ringed in black is the odd one out.

PAGE 82

PAGE 83

There are 11 adults and 8 chicks.

PAGE 84

PAGE 85